LEGEND MEETS TRUTH
Bigfoot in Rhode Island

Dina M. Palazini

Copyright © 2013 by Dina M. Palazini
All rights reserved.

No part of this publication may be reproduced in any form or by any means, without the prior permission in writing from the author.

ISBN-13: 978-1481140621
ISBN-10: 1481140620

Cover artwork by Thomas Finley
Cover and book design by Kris Stepney
Edited by Katherine Viveiros-Lachut

For more information about the author, visit:
www.BeyondTheVeilParanormal.com
www.BigfootSeekers.com
www.BigRhodey.com

**This book is dedicated to
my daughter Savannah
and my son Austin.**

LEGEND MEETS TRUTH

Artwork by Thomas Finley

PREFACE
Behind Every Legend Lies Some Truth

Native American Indians have passed down through generations their accounts of this creature we now call Bigfoot. There have been reports dating back over 2,500 years of creatures that people just can't explain. Could this be the missing link, or just a figment of the imagination?

As we explore deeper into the realm of the unknown, there is so much more to be discovered when it comes to finding answers about UFO's, Loch Ness Monsters, the Jersey Devil, Yeti, Bigfoot, etc. The phenomenon surrounding encounters with unidentified creatures and the mystical beings have fascinated cryptozoologists and researchers alike for centuries. As we explore further with some scientific depth and analysis we can uncover the truth behind the legends.

Who is this creature we call Bigfoot? I have heard many names and terms for the Big Guy -- Sasquatch, Grassman, Skunk Ape, Skookum, Woolybooger, Man Monkey and many more. I have met many researchers in the Bigfoot field, most are respected and some not so much. The majority of us however; we are here to untangle the myths and legends, document evidence of Bigfoot, and prove its existence. We are not in any way out to harm or exploit this creature, but to protect and preserve their habitat. After seeing this beautiful being for myself, I know that this is not an ape, but more man than anything. This was my observation at the time of my sighting and not scientific fact.

LEGEND MEETS TRUTH

People question their own sanity after seeing this creature for the first time and most will not talk to anyone about what they had seen for fear of humiliation and ridicule.

Is there a missing link? Scientists have often wondered how to define the "missing link". Where did it go? Is the missing link right here in our own backyard? I believe this crea-

Photograph by Kris Stepney, 2012

ture is homosapien and could very well be the missing link to modern man or another species of man not yet discovered by the scientific community.

This book is based on both eyewitness accounts and theory. There is no real solid evidence that this creature exists, but we are getting closer.

Bigfoot in Rhode Island

Many people have said to me that Rhode Island isn't big enough to sustain such a large creature as Bigfoot. They say that the state is too small for this being to thrive and remain elusive. There is a lot of state forest and uninhabited land here; plenty of space for this creature to live and remain unseen. Eyewitnesses have come forward with claims to have seen Bigfoot right here in the smallest state. I am determined to prove that Bigfoot lives and breathes here. I know for a fact that they do. How do I know? Because I came face to face with one!

Undisclosed

There are a few locations I choose to keep undisclosed from the public. I don't want to reveal these areas for fear of some trigger happy person who may want to harm them. I also don't want to expose these locations where I do my research because of possible contamination. It is my goal to protect Bigfoot and try to get a law passed that would fine or give jail time to those who harm them.

LEGEND MEETS TRUTH

Photograph by Dina Palazini, 2012

The Critics and Non-Believers

If it were not for the critics and non-believers and the questions they ask, we as researchers would look at the Bigfoot phenomena with a narrow and subjective viewpoint. They open us up to essential scrutiny of the evidence we collect to help prove of their existence.

Legends of Bigfoot

There are a number of legends about the creature we call Bigfoot and stories that have been passed down for generations. Some of these legends fade away, but most are kept alive through the accounts of true eyewitnesses. There are countless amounts of people that have heard about Bigfoot and some believe he lives right here in North America. It is a fascination for us as humans to think that this man- like creature exists. Does he exist? There is evidence that brings us closer to finding the truth. Does this creature live only in North America?

There are many legends and eyewitness reports all over the world. For instance, the Yeti is said to be a man-like creature that has been seen in the Himalayan mountains and are sacred in both Buddhism and Hinduism. The Yeti, sometimes called the Abominable Snowman or Meh-tec, are names commonly used by the indigenous people. This creature is believed to be taller than the average human and has similar characteristics of the North American Bigfoot. *(1)* This is a big part of their culture, mythology and lore. Rhode Island has many reports of this creature dating back to early Native American legends to present day.

LEGEND MEETS TRUTH

Map from www.geology.com

Rhode Island – History and Habitat

Although Rhode Island is the smallest state in the union, 59 percent of its land is forest with nearly 393,000 acres. Much of this forest land is privately owned, leaving around 25 percent preserved as state owned. It borders to the east of Connecticut and to the south and west of Massachusetts. It is home to many woodland animals such as deer, coyote, wild turkey, fisher cat, beaver and bear. Much of the trees found in the area are oak, maple, pine and birch. *(2)*

Rhode Island has a deep history that goes back to Native American roots. It is the land originally inhabited by native tribes such as the Wampanoag, Narragansett, Nipmuc, Pequot and Niantic. Much of the history of the Native American people has been lost after Roger Williams' arrival in the 1600's and after the King Phillip's War in 1675 to 1678. *(3)* There are legends that have been passed down from generations of Bigfoot encounters with the Native American people. Some tell of a white-haired Bigfoot. It has been said that the Native Americans viewed this creature as a spiritual being.

The Bigfoot Closet

I had been in the so-called Bigfoot closet for many years, it was very traumatic to me when I saw this creature. People have asked how can you block something like this out of your mind for so long? I believe it was post-traumatic stress disorder (PTSD). This event had frightened me to the core, and like most people that have been in a war or have had something happen to them that scared them into post-traumatic stress, it only takes a trigger to bring it all back, and this was mine.

The Memory Trigger

One evening, Carl Johnson the co-founder of my group Beyond the Veil Paranormal Research (founded in June 2009) came over to discuss a paranormal case that we were working on. The History Channel was on the TV in the background as we talked about some of the work that we were doing at the time. This particular show was about Bigfoot. I knew some things about the creature but was not paying any attention to the show as it was airing. There was something eerie about this particular show that just triggered the memory of something that I had blocked out for a long time.

As Carl was talking, I said under my breath, "I've seen one of those." I started shaking and felt sick to my stomach. He stopped talking mid-sentence and looked at me. Carl could see that I was distressed. He said, "What?" I repeated, "Yeah, I saw one of those." Then I broke down and started to cry. Carl didn't know what was going on. He tried to comfort me and was trying to calm me down. It took me some time that night to come to my senses. He had asked me to tell him more but I just couldn't. I could see the whole scenario playing out in my mind about that night and I had to decline. This was my own private nightmare. I told him that I was not ready to talk about what I saw in the woods that night. He understood and dropped the subject.

Although this intrigued Carl and I trusted him, I just didn't trust anybody when it came to the terror I felt that warm summer night. A few months later when I finally had the nerve to tell him about what I had seen, it was like a big weight was lifted off my shoulders.

Photograph by Dina Palazini, 2012

Bigfoot in Rhode Island

In April of 2010, Carl and I were asked to speak about our work in the paranormal field at the Queen City Para-Con. This was a great event and many friends were made. It was at this event where I had met Don Keating. He had a casting of a huge footprint, and I was mesmerized. I had to touch this footprint casting and introduce myself to him. I felt comfortable talking to Don because of the fact he is in the Bigfoot field and has experience. I proceeded to tell him about how I had seen Bigfoot in Rhode Island. I gave him a brief description of my story. I didn't know Don well enough to want tell him my whole story.

Photograph by Kris Stepney, 2012

When he stood up to give his lecture that evening, he mentioned that there were two states without any reports of Bigfoot sightings; Hawaii and Rhode Island. I spoke up and said in front of his audience, "Um... not anymore." Then Don said, "Till now!" I felt I had made a good friend that night.

Big Rhodey Research Project

In August 2010, I founded the Big Rhodey Research Project. The term Big Rhodey is a play on Rhode Island's popular nickname 'Little Rhody'. As far as we're concerned, once the creature we call Bigfoot crosses into the boundaries of Rhode Island, it becomes 'Big Rhodey' and remains so while it's here.

Forming this group was my way of expressing and documenting some of my testimony and also to further my research. Since it's development, I have met a lot of Bigfoot enthusiasts and many reports have been forwarded to us through the website. This is a small group of people with good credentials. I don't like big crowds or groups. The Big Rhodey Research Project is a group of everyday folks that want to research more about this creature. We explore with the understanding that we need to be patient and stay open-minded and know that they could be watching us.

Don Keating's Visit to Rhode Island

In September of 2010, Don Keating and his wife Missy had taken a trip to Rhode Island for a visit. They were very interested to see the location where I had my sighting. Don and Missy had gone out in the field with me that day and we explored the area. After their visit, Don expressed an interest in having me speak at his conference that he was holding the following year, the 23rd Annual Ohio Bigfoot Conference. I was a bit apprehensive about the thought of speaking in front of an audience about my experience but I looked at it as an opportunity to meet other people in the Bigfoot community and to see Don and Missy again. I knew it would also bring awareness about Bigfoot's existence in Rhode Island.

Speaking Publicly About My Sighting

Upon speaking at the 23rd Annual Bigfoot Conference held at Salt Fork State Park in Ohio on May 14th 2011, I was very apprehensive about talking about my experience for the first time. I had never even spoken about this to my own mother, never mind in front of over a thousand people that I have never seen before! Shaky and sick to my stomach, I asked Don if I could speak first so I could just get it over with and hide in my hotel room for the rest of the conference. Trembling inside, I approached the podium and just began to tell my story about what happened on that particular evening.

My Testimony

I was 17 years old in the summer of 1984. It was a warm day when three of my friends and I decided to take the top down on the convertible and go for a ride. It was around dusk when we headed to our favorite road in Cumberland, Rhode Island, known to be haunted by the locals. We had cruised that road often and had seen some strange things, but nothing could top what we saw and experienced that night!

We pulled off to the side of the road just so we could hang out and talk, just being teenagers. I remember that the driver had pulled over onto the wrong side. I knew that this was wrong because I was studying for my drivers licence at the time.

Dina, in her teens, circa 1984

I was sitting behind the driver's seat closest to the woods. As we laughed and joked amongst ourselves I could smell something rancid. I just thought, "Well its the woods", and forgot about it. The smell had then gotten stronger and I got the eerie feeling that something was watching us. It just seemed odd that night, there were no crickets or birds chirping. It was eerily quiet. Still feeling like something was watching us, I turned and looked to my left and saw a very big hairy man-like creature and started to scream. The guys saw this at about the same time and we all were screaming. "What the f--k is that?!" "Get out of here!" "What is that!?" I was so scared that I was trying to crawl under the seat of the car. I can't even begin to describe the feeling, it was pure horror. The driver was stumbling to get the car started for what seemed like forever. When he finally did, we were racing down this narrow road, surprised we didn't get killed just getting out of there. As we approached the end of the road, we got back on the main street and saw a police car go by. We were in hot pursuit of this poor cop. We were beeping the horn and flashing the high beams to pull him over. Not too many teenagers often pull over a cop! He finally pulled over and came up to us in the car. He could see we were crying and we started screaming that we saw a monster in the woods. This poor guy, he didn't know what we were thinking. He just knew that we were terrified. He said to calm down and he would check it out. I never heard back from the officer, and my friends and I lost touch soon after that evening. I believe it was because it was so traumatic for us all.

It took me over twenty years to talk about that night, but after telling my story in front of all those people in the audience at the lecture, they made me feel so comfortable and were so open and down to earth. This was the right place to be to talk about my Bigfoot experience. I made a lot of friends that weekend and we still keep in touch to this day.

Since I have talked and lectured about Bigfoot, more and more eyewitnesses have come to me and told me of similar accounts that they have experienced. One report was in the 1980's and one just recently in 2012 on the same road where I had my sighting.

Q & A

Q: How did you know it was a male?
A: Well, he wasn't wearing jeans. I was at eye level in the car and I could see that it was male. I could see genitalia.

Q: What were you wearing? Did you have on perfume or hairspray?
A: It was the 80's and I bought stock in Aqua Net, so yes I am sure I was wearing hair spray and perfume.

Q: Do you think this creature is inter-dimensional?
A: Personally I don't believe that Bigfoot is inter-dimensional. I believe they are biological, but it could be possible. I really don't know.

Q: What color was the car and did it have a loud exhaust?
A: The car was blue. It was parked and wasn't running. We were sitting in the car talking to each other for about fifteen minutes before we saw him.

Q: What did it smell like?
A: It smelled awful. It's hard to describe the smell; something like body odor and wet dog.

Q: How did you know it was a Bigfoot and not a bear?

A: It is rare to see bear in Rhode Island. That doesn't mean that they are not here, but black bears are not eight feet tall. This looked like a very large man covered in hair.

Q: Could it have been a man in a monkey suit?
A: The road we were on is a quiet, wooded road not traveled much, so what would a man be doing in a monkey suit waiting for some teenagers that just so happen to park at that particular spot in hopes to scare the daylights out of them? It just doesn't seem likely.

Q: Were you on your menstrual cycle?
A: I can't remember. It is possible because it is a monthly occurrence.

People do come out with some interesting questions and they all are important. They make you think outside the box. At the time I saw this creature, it scared me half to death. I was a young girl and didn't really know what I was looking at, at the time; I know now. I remember this creature was very tall and very wide – bigger than any football player. This creature didn't seem to want to hurt us. I think he was curious – observing and watching.

Just like you never forget your first love, well you never forget your first Bigfoot. It was very emotional and scary, and it is embedded deep in my mind. This is something I will never forget. Ever.

The Big Rhodey Expedition

On July 24, 2010, good friends and colleagues Greg Best, Kris Stepney, and two other friends joined me in a Rhode Island Bigfoot expedition. They wanted to film my testimony and see the area where I had seen this creature. I normally do not bring people to the site, but I trusted them with confidence. I always like to take the lead when I go out in the field because I look for prints and most people don't look down when they are walking. As we all headed up the trail head I pointed out to Greg and the rest of the group to what looked like a big human-like footprint. Greg proceeded to film but I could see that he couldn't believe what he was looking at. Being a professional in his field, he just kept filming. We spent a few hours out there that day and found a few more. They had been there for awhile and were

Greg Best and Dina Palazini examine footprints.
Photograph by Kris Stepney, 2010

LEGEND MEETS TRUTH

Dina Palazini, Rosemary Ellen Guiley and Carl Johnson prepare for a Bigfoot expedition

Photograph by Greg Best, 2010

not deep enough to cast the print. There wouldn't have had any distinctive dermal ridges, but it was a good find anyway. We have gone back out there on a few occasions.

Around the same time we were out doing research, we had been in contact with prolific author Rosemary Ellen Guiley. We were discussing about Bigfoot in the area and she had asked if she could come along on an expedition. She wanted to see the area where I had my sighting as well as interview me about what I had seen that summer in 1984. She is a very intelligent and down to earth woman.

On August 8th, 2010, we brought Rosemary to the undisclosed area where I had seen the creature. We did see some partial prints but nothing that was good enough to cast. I think the big guy had left the area and hasn't been around for a while. Just as well, the land is up for sale now.

Open-minded Exploration
by Kris Stepney

It is difficult for many people to believe that Bigfoot exists. I have been asked many times why I believe this creature is out there when I have not yet seen one. I suppose what drives me to find the answer as to its existence is simply curiosity. I haven't seen one, but I have seen evidence of what I believe might hold clues to their existence. I have heard other people tell of their accounts, and I don't believe these people would put themselves out there to endure the questioning and the ridicule from others, if they weren't so certain about what they experienced. Only when we begin to question what's out there can we begin to find answers.

When I am out in the field looking for evidence of Bigfoot, I go with an open mind. Something as simple as a rock placed in a path, or sticks formed together in an unnatural way – I don't immediately assume it was a Bigfoot doing these things, but I also do not simply pass it off either. Going in with an open mind means looking at the whole picture and considering all possibilities. Being a paranormal investigator, I was trained to first try to debunk anything out of the ordinary and try to come up with a rational explanation. Using my inner human instincts also helps me to keep me open to finding answers to the unexplained.

Some people feel that relying on instincts does not help to provide answers, but leaves room for human error because it is simply a "feeling" and not tangible proof. However, I think listening to your instincts plays an important role in researching because it helps keep you open to discovering things that you might have otherwise overlooked. I know that explaining to someone that I felt like I was being watched while out exploring the woods is not enough proof to say it was a Bigfoot, and I agree. But getting that feeling is also part of what drives me to want to find out more. There is a lot in this world that I believe has yet to be discovered. Only when we get out there and explore can we begin to find answers. So when I am asked if I believe Bigfoot exists, my answer to that is that anything is possible. This is why I am in the field of Bigfoot research.

Women and Bigfoot

On June 4, 2011, Kris and I decided to go on a weekend expedition and do a little researching on our own. We headed to Bellingham, Massachusetts. A good friend of mine had given us access to their land that was attached to a Massachusetts state forest. It was really nice because of the fact that there were no people out there and we could feel comfortable doing some primitive camping. We packed up the four-wheeler with our gear and headed quite a few miles out. We set up camp, made a small fire pit, then started looking for any kind of animal prints just to see what wildlife was in the area. We found deer and coyote tracks, however they were not fresh and looked like they had been there for awhile.

We gathered our wood for the night, sat by the fire, and I decided to do some wood knocking. Around 12:30 am, to my surprise, there was a response. Kris' eyes got really wide and she said, "I think you just invoked a Bigfoot." So I did a little more wood knocking, but heard nothing. At around 2:00 a.m., Kris and I could smell a pungent odor, which was a very familiar smell for me. I've smelled this stink before. Oh boy... here we go! I'm not going to say that I wasn't nervous because I was. I had to keep saying to myself that if he wanted to hurt me, he would have in 1984. I needed to stay calm for Kris. She had never seen one of these creatures. Kris began filming in night vision.

The fire was dying out and the wood reserve was getting low. Earlier that day Kris had asked if we should get some firewood at the grocery store, I laughed at her and called her a silly girl. I said "We are going to be in the woods, there is plenty of wood!" I should have listened to her. So we had to go out there and get more wood. We really didn't want to, but we had no choice. We had steak and corn on the cob to cook for dinner. Reluctantly, we headed out with one flashlight and a night vision camera and gathered some more wood. It was surprisingly cold that night for it being June, in the low 40's, so it was a good thing we did. We had the fire blazing again and then we both looked at each other and I asked Kris, "Can you feel that?" It felt like something was watching us. As we were scanning the woods we noticed we could see eye shine, it was about 8 feet up near the trees. This was something that was big and tall. We felt like we were surrounded. Kris whispered, "There is something behind us." Just then, we heard a loud crash. We

Kris Stepney by the campfire.

both screamed in surprise at the sound that broke the silence of the woods. Shaking in our shoes, we started laughing. This was why we were out here, it's just Bigfoot. I didn't believe this creature was going to hurt us.

I know for a fact that this wasn't a deer, or even a black bear. It sounded like a big thick branch that was snapped, as if something very large stepped on it or had broken it off a tree. Needless to say, I really didn't want to cook the steak and corn, but I did it anyway without any further adieu. Kris and I didn't go to sleep until dawn. We were just a couple of women in the woods primitive camping for the weekend and looking for Bigfoot. Be careful what you go out searching for, because you just might find it. Or in this case, it just might find you.

Kris Stepney and Aryes Clague exploring the woods in South County, Rhode Island

Photograph by Dina Palazini, 2012

LEGEND MEETS TRUTH

Dina Palazini riding Throttle; heading out with the Bigfoot Seekers
Photograph by Kris Stepney, 2012

Bigfoot Seekers

In April 2012, I founded Bigfoot Seekers. This is a Bigfoot research group comprised of just women with co-founders Kris Stepney and Aryes Clague. We had the theory that women are less threatening to this being. My belief is that Bigfoot is empathic and has the ability to sense if someone wants to harm them. This creature is very intelligent and will only show itself to certain people. Being empathic, maybe it can sense that. I am a lover of the four-legged and the two-legged. As a child, I had the ability to earn the trust of wild animals and hand feed them; skunks, raccoons, squirrels, birds, etc. I believe my team members to have the same ability. Kris is the quiet one with a great heart and spirit and Aryes has the ability to sense and feel things that most people choose to ignore. I also call Aryes the Horse Whisperer. She has such a way with these animals and it truly amazes me. As a team, we work very well together and often go out on horseback to cover more ground. There is so much land and forest here in Rhode Island that we could go for days without ever seeing another human being.

On June 29, 2012 around noontime, Aryes was out riding her horse Godiva. It had rained earlier that morning so the ground was still a little damp. She called me on her cell phone, frantic, I couldn't recognize her voice at all. She was so shaky and she was crying. She said, "I just saw Bigfoot!" I was stunned. "What did you say?" I asked. She repeated, "I just saw Bigfoot!" I couldn't believe it! My heart starting racing. I asked her to please go see if there were any prints. She rode her horse up to the rock where she had seen the Bigfoot sitting down. She said there were partial prints, human-like but much bigger. I called Kris and we raced down to the location

LEGEND MEETS TRUTH

Bigfoot Seekers – Kris Stepney, Dina Palazini, and Aryes Clague
Photograph by Savannah Palazini, 2012

with the casting powder, measuring tape, and video camera in hand. By the time we got there it was late in the afternoon and the temperature outside was about 98 degrees with very high humidity. The hill we had to climb wasn't easy, as it was very rocky with a lot of soft sand and big boulders. It was no easy task, but as researchers in this field, it really never is. This property is connected to state forest and preserves. There is a lot of ground out there for a Bigfoot to live. Are they right in her backyard? They very well could be.

Rock Signs

On September 22, 2012, after a night of rain, Kris and I decided to go to an undisclosed area that we normally frequent. There have been some sightings at this location and this was the place where I had cast my first print. Was it a Bigfoot print? Well, I wasn't entirely sure. We measured it at around 15 inches long and had human-like width to the print. It didn't seem wide enough to be Bigfoot, but who would be out here in the middle of nowhere without shoes? It didn't make any sense to me. The terrain is rocky and some trails are gravel. There are also some areas of mud. It is so far out in the forest that I just couldn't see a human out there without shoes. I was thinking perhaps it could have been a juvenile Bigfoot? I really don't know for certain.

I have been out there a few times with my small team of three or four, but on this one particular day in September, Kris and I went out there to hike and look for some more prints. On the trail head, we noticed that there was a big rock that seemed out of place. We looked at each other and were dumbfounded! This was a big dirty rock just there in the middle of the trail. It had rained the night before! All of the rocks were rain clean. This was a dirty rock that appeared to be just unearthed. By what? I have no clue.

Kris and I looked around, still dumbfounded. Where did it come from? As we looked closer at the dirty rock, we saw that there was a very large footprint next to it. It was hard to see at first, but then the sun shifted just enough for us to see the toes, the width and the length. It measured at about 16 inches in length and 7 inches in width. There was just one print there, we were baffled at that. We had searched all over

LEGEND MEETS TRUTH

the trail and into the adjacent woods to see if there was a hole that was dug out. We were not able to find anything. It was like the big guy just wanted to let us know he or she was there. The print was too shallow to cast and I didn't have my casting square to contain it; however we did get some great pictures of the print. Unfortunately, this was a day trip, and I don't take all my gear on that day trips; although, I'm thinking I should take it all every time. Now I know. You can never predict when you will find evidence. Always take your equipment and casting powder. All in all It was a good day in the field.

The dirty rock in the middle of the trail.

The Cavern

Early October 2012, a friend and colleague of mine (who asked to remain anonymous) and I went back to the area where I had my first encounter with Bigfoot. He and I decided to go off trail for the first two hours of our hike. The terrain has a lot of ledge, big boulders, and quite a few caverns. One of these caverns is very large and deep with two points of entry. This cavern is definitely big enough to provide shelter for a large creature; bear or even a Bigfoot. We looked around for awhile but didn't see any sign of anything living there for some time. We decided to hike on a trail going toward the exact place where I had seen the creature. It was very quiet and still that day, not even a bird chirping. We looked around and took some photos but there was no evidence of the big guy. Being at the place where I had my encounter was eerie and I was filled with the anticipation that I would see him again

Cave system discovered during 2010 expedition.

LEGEND MEETS TRUTH

Dina explores the cavern.

BIGFOOT IN RHODE ISLAND

LEGEND MEETS TRUTH

Great Swamp

Upon researching Bigfoot sightings in Rhode Island, I have come across some reports of Bigfoot at Great Swamp in the West Kingston Management Area. These sightings date back to the early 1600's by Native American tribes. Legend has it that the creature was very large, about 8 feet tall, and covered in white hair. There have been recent reports to this date describing very similar accounts. I have tried to get in touch with those eyewitnesses for an interview with no avail.

Great Swamp covers a total land area of 3349 acres. There are 2262 acres of wetlands, 897 acres of forest cover, 88 acres of agricultural land, and 102 acres of brush, utilities etc. The

Great Swamp.
Photograph by Dina Palazini, 2012

area contains extensive forested freshwater wetlands, dominated by red maple swamps with some cedar swamp. *(4)*

It was a warm day for November of 2012 when the girls and I decided to go to Great Swamp. We were very excited to be researching that day, because of all the reports of Bigfoot sightings in the area. We had never researched this site before and there is a vast amount of land to explore. Well, to my disappointment it was crawling with people – hikers, hunters, bike riders and dogs. We should have taken the horses that day to cover more ground and to get away from human contamination. There were plenty of deer tracks in the muddy areas, but also human tracks as well. I do believe that Bigfoot could be living in this area just because of the amount of land and food resources there. But you're most likely not going to see this creature here because there are just too many people walking around. My team and I will not be going back unless we have access through private land.

Walking along the trail, Great Swamp
Photograph by Kris Stepney, 2012

Possible Baby Footprint

It was a warm day on November 23, 2012. Kris, myself, and my daughter Savannah decided to go to my secret hot spot. This is the same location where I had found and cast my first what I believe to be a Bigfoot print. The three of us were walking along the trail and taking pictures of the scenery. As

I looked down to avoid falling over a rock, I saw what looked to me like an oversized bare footprint. Then my daughter said, "Hey Mom, I found a print too!" It was a baby footprint with a bigger one right beside it. I took out the measuring tape and the bigger print was 15 inches long and 7 inches in width. The smaller print was 9 inches long and 4 inches in width. They were both in a very soft, sandy place on the trail. I wanted to do a cast of them, but I really didn't think it would be a good cast because of the soft sand. It was an exciting find for us that day.

Personal Accounts and Testimonies

I seem to be finding more and more reports on this elusive creature we call Bigfoot here in Rhode Island. All of these reports are very similar in nature. Some of the reports that I mention are from eyewitnesses who have contacted me directly and wanted to share their encounter. Others were reported on various Bigfoot research websites. It is somewhat comforting to know that I am not the only one to have had an experience.

Washington County Sighting

This sighting from an anonymous eyewitness was reported on the GCBRO website detailing a possible Bigfoot encounter on Perry Avenue in South Kingstown, Rhode Island one evening in September of 1975. As this man was riding his bike from his girlfriends house back to the URI campus, he encountered what he believes was a Bigfoot. While trying to fix the pedal on his bike, he heard what sounded like very heavy, crushing steps from something that was bipedal. The sound grew closer and heavier and he felt that whatever it was, it sounded huge. He fixed his bike and proceeded on his way. As he was heading down the street, a huge figure steps into the road about twenty to twenty-five feet away from him. He described the creature as being around 400 to 450 pounds. It was "standing with arms straight down bent over on its knuckles" and the creature's knees were slightly bent. The physical features he noticed was that this being had enormous arms and legs, close-set eyes, a wide, human-like nose, and that the back of its head was higher than the front. He could see that this creature had black hair that went from its mouth down to about its chest, and that there was very little hair on the being's chest. This creature stared at him momentarily before proceeding to chase him down the street for about ten yards. As he made his way up the street, he stopped to turn around and watched as the creature turned and jumped over a nearby rock wall. *(5)*

LEGEND MEETS TRUTH

This next story is very compelling to me because it hits home. Cody Ray and I had met at a paranormal conference here in Rhode Island. He is a young man that has a passion for the paranormal. 'Paranormal' is a term meaning out of the ordinary. It's something that you do not see everyday or can easily explain with scientific proof. I could really feel his energy when I met him. He is a sincere young man and has nothing to lose by writing his story. He had confessed to me that he had a very frightening experience on the same road where I had my sighting!

Cumberland Sighting
By Cody Ray DesBiens

The night of August 26th, 2011 still runs through my head every time I drive by that certain road in Rhode Island. My name is Cody Ray DesBiens and I have been a supernatural researcher for a few years now. Not only do I study spirits but I also investigate Unidentified Flying Objects (UFO) and Bigfoot or Sasquatch type mammals.

I had heard stories about this road being "haunted" so I originally went there that night investigating paranormal activity. My intentions were definitely not set on hunting down a Sasquatch or seeing one because I really had no interest in them at that time. I remember pulling my car over on the side of the road where activity was said to be. It isn't a busy road at all so there were only a few cars that had passed by that night. I remember feeling a very peaceful but mysterious feeling throughout the night. Keep in mind that this road is in the middle of nowhere and is surrounded by forest with no homes in the area, so I was alone with no cell phone service. About ten minutes into my investigation it was extremely quiet until I heard the very distinct loud sound of branches snapping. I also heard some shuffling of leaves and dirt like something was taking footsteps.

Whatever it was, it was very big with long legs because the sound of each step he was taking were spread further apart if one of us was to walk. It takes us about one second for our foot to lift from the ground and take a step while we are walking. This creature had his steps spread double the time as we do which gives me one reason why he is big and bipedal. I also believe he was large because of the stomping each step was making. The sound I heard were not twigs breaking, these were big branches snapping. I heard this thing take about four steps until it emerged from the thick woods to the edge of the road about fifty feet away from me. I distinctly remember that the creature did not step onto the road; it stayed a few steps back.

There are only one or two street lights on this road and I wasn't near any of them. I only had a little flashlight that couldn't reach to where this thing was. I was only able to see a blurry outline of a figure of something I know I had never seen before. The best way I can describe it is that it looked big and strong. Being in the middle of nowhere with no cell phone service, I ran back to my car and flew out of there. I had my video camera in my hand that night and didn't realize it was still recording but like I said the lighting was terrible and I was at a good distance away from the creature so I only caught the slight sound of the footsteps.

I've been back to that same location about ten times after that night hoping the same thing will happen again, but it hasn't yet. I haven't told this story to too many people because

I just consider it data to add to the theory that these creatures do exist. I am a part of this field to find the truth about supernatural things. I'm certainly not in this to make a skeptic a believer. When you have an experience happen like this in front of you, it's burned into your head for the rest of your life no matter if you like it or not. I have nothing to gain by telling one of my testimonies, only the fact that I'm that much closer to finding out the truth of what's in those woods.

This is on the same road where Dina had her sighting. Is Bigfoot out there? I really think he is.

George Washington Management Area

The George Washington Management Area is located in Northern Rhode Island near the Connecticut border. With nearly 3489 acres of area, it is primarily forest land with 439 square foot of wetlands. This location provides camping, hiking, fishing, and boating for people to enjoy. *(6)* But might it also be home to Bigfoot? There have been documented sightings of Bigfoot in this area.

When my team went to explore the area, we found that there were a lot of people there and it seemed to be too busy of a place for us to do any conducive research. Along most of the paths we took, we could hear people nearby and the ground was heavily contaminated with human footprints. That's not to say that because we have yet to find evidence in this area, that it's not possible for this creature to exist here.

One sighting reported in the area was from Jeff (last name

omitted). He stated that late one evening in July of 2002, while on a two-hour walk through the park, he had an encounter with what he believes to be a Bigfoot. He first noticed an unusual smell similar to that of rotten meat. Assuming it was perhaps some sort of dead animal, he didn't take much notice of it and carried on. Then he heard a strange scream that sounded like it came from that of a monkey or a gorilla, but very low in tone and very loud. This scared him and he picked up his pace to head back to his car. The sound continued as he made his way down the path, and it continued to get louder as he went on. When he heard the sound of tree limbs snapping, he panicked and ran the rest of the way to his car. He got in his car and proceeded to head out of the park as quickly as he could. As he was leaving, with the car headlights he could see a big figure in the road up ahead. He didn't believe this was a bear, as the figure appeared to be 7 to 8 feet tall and probably around 300 pounds. He described it as being covered with dark brown hair with some bald patches and looked human-like. As he came upon it, the creature screamed once more and then ran into the woods. The way it moved and ran appeared to be that of a man, but he didn't believe this was a man. Because of what he experienced, he is now apprehensive to return to this area alone at night. *(7)*

Pine Grove Cemetery Sighting
By Greg Best

I am the lead member of Oracle Paranormal Research Society, an experienced paranormal research group. In the summer of 2011, my team of six and I were on an investigation at Pine Grove Cemetery in Coventry Rhode Island. We had special permission that night to be in the cemetery after dusk. It was very late - after midnight. While four of the members were off in a different area investigating, my teammate Julie and I were in the far corner of the cemetery filming. This cemetery is surrounded by a lot of woods and many of the headstones are back a ways in the woods. While we were filming, Julie noticed something red shining about 25 to 30 feet from where we were standing. I turned and began filming. The red shine was so bright, it almost looked like a bike reflector. At first, I could only see one, and it was low to the ground almost like it was sitting. I began to walk towards it with my camera steady on the reflection. Suddenly it began to rise, and as it did, it didn't go straight up, but kind of wavered as it stood. Now I could clearly see two red eyes, about 7-1/2 feet high. I kept walking towards it and suddenly heard a loud snapping sound of a limb that was probably a good 3" thick, and then it was gone. We didn't hear any other sounds, it was just gone. Was this Bigfoot? I believe it was.

Sighting in Diamond Hill State Park
By Dylan Fuller

I was sitting at the computer and my brother came running into the room. He said he saw something big and white in the field out back, so I went to see what it was. I saw just a little white dot move in the woods so I said it was just a deer. But my other brother said "Dylan, turn around." When I did, I saw this 7 to 8 foot tall monstrous creature standing there at the edge of the woods. I was speechless. I watched it walk through the field, jump over the dirt road leading to the vineyard, then crouch down behind a fallen tree. I had my brothers go in the house while I went to see what this thing was. I grabbed my knife and walked through my yard to where it was standing but when I got about ten feet away, I just couldn't get myself to go any further. My heart was racing so I turned around and walked back to the house – more scared than I've ever been in my life. I watched this creature for about half an hour longer until I decided to go inside. The last I saw, it had moved from one fallen tree to another.

The next day, I went outback to go follow its tracks. At this point, I didn't know what it was. I called my father asking him what he thought it might have been, but he had no clue. I never thought of it as being a Sasquatch until I followed its path and found fourteen and a half inch foot prints all the way from where we first saw it to where it crouched down.

Diamond Hill State Park. Photo by Dina Palazini, 2012

LEGEND MEETS TRUTH

The prints had five distinct toes and one of the prints was at least an inch and a half deep into the mud. I never believed in Bigfoot until I saw this creature in 2011 just after Thanksgiving. I never would have thought there were Bigfoot in Rhode Island, but when I thought about it, why wouldn't there be?

Dina casts a print.

Bones

There has been no evidence of bones. I believe it is because these creatures are highly intelligent and bury their dead with a marker only they would recognize. Just as we humans bury and mourn our dead, my belief, as well as some researchers, feel this is their way to stay hidden from people and the desecration of their dead family members.

Many Bigfoot researchers and biologists alike have gone in the field for days and weeks at a time and have rarely come across a carcass of any animals. Unless it is a fresh kill or a recent natural death of the animal, the stages of decomposition can vary due to climate. There are five stages of decomposition: Fresh, Bloat, Active and Advanced Decay, and Dry Decay. Decomposition is coupled with two stages: Chemical decomposition: Autolysis and Putrefaction. These two stages contribute to the chemical process of decomposition, which breaks down all of the main components of the body. *(8)* As long with scavengers and the rate of decomposition, it is very rare to find remains.

There have been reports of Bigfoot in every state in the nation except for Hawaii and until recently, Rhode Island. As far as I know, this big hairy man-like creature cannot read road signs.

Physical Characteristics
By Carl L. Johnson

Bigfoot is most known for the tracks it leaves; hence the name. This seems to be the most frequently reported evidence of the creature. The footprints basically appear to be human, but in general are oversized and rather wedge-shaped, lacking much of an arch indent and perhaps structured to support considerable weight for the biped stride. It is significant to note that the foot does not have an extended big toe, separated from the other four toes on each foot. All of the great apes: Gorillas, Chimpanzees, Bonobos and Orangutans have extended big toes resembling thumbs, for grasping when they climb. This suggests a closer kinship to our species. In most reported sightings, Bigfoot consistently walks erect. The spines and pelvic girdle would have to be very humanlike, tough sturdier to accommodate greater body weight with massive musculature. Neanderthals, our distant European cousins who went extinct around 29,000 years ago (though some researchers in Siberia would argue the point!) had denser bones than modern Homo Sapiens, but they were on the average of shorter stature than are we. Their stockiness and barrel chests were quite probably adaptations to ice age conditions. An earlier form of human, Homo Erectus, possessed a smaller brain case than we do -- Neanderthals averaged larger than ours yet somewhat differently shaped -- but would tend to be tall; males often achieving heights of over six feet. Homo Erectus must have been excellent long-distance runners. They probably were the first to harness fire. The two basic categories I've named are presently thought not to be directly ancestral to modern humans, although we are related. They illustrate species, including our own, have offshoots, and living creatures adapt to their environments. As with the feet, Bigfoot's hands are very similar to ours, though the level of dexterity is speculative. Bigfoot's physiognomy, the face, well... from what is described, you could take an overlay image of a reconstruction of Neanderthal: the quintessential caveman, combine that with an overlay image of reconstructed Homo Erectus, and you'll produce a portrait of what many folks will recognize as Bigfoot! Neanderthals most likely had capacity for at least rudimentary speech, this assumption predicated on the positioning of a hyoid bone located behind the larynx as found in Neanderthal remains. Homo Erectus might have mumbled some phonetics. There exist a few purported examples of recorded Bigfoot speech. Certainly these recordings are amusing, and having listened, I feel not all can be dismissed as hoaxes.

Bigfoot and Horse Hair Braiding

There have been some reports that Bigfoot has braided horses manes and tails. Campers taking their horses out for weekend camping trips have often reported that when they woke up in the morning they had found that some of their horses had their manes or tails braided during the night. The horses never spooked and the campers didn't hear a sound. They also reported that the braid was very primitive in nature. The campers were baffled by this.

Rock Throwing

Why does Bigfoot throw rocks? Nobody really knows. The theory is when a human approaches their territory the creature feels threatened and is letting you know that you need to leave.

LEGEND MEETS TRUTH

Dina listens with a parabolic dish.

I have had that experience in June 2012, while my female team and I were down In Hope Valley Rhode Island. We had gone out on the horses that day just to see if the big guy was around. We didn't see or hear anything that day so we put the horses up for the night and had a little camp fire. The girls and I were just sitting around laughing and talking, when suddenly we heard something lurking in the woods. It seemed like they were all around us . What was all around us? I really don't know. I was thinking maybe the coyotes were out prowling that night, so we just stayed close to the fire and continued on with our conversation. Suddenly I saw a small stone go past me and then it happened again. It was almost like this creature was trying to get our attention. None of the stones or pebbles hit us. Needless to say it was an interesting night.

Vocalizations

In the field of Bigfoot study and research, people have heard strange vocalizations – howls, whistles and grunts. Knowing most of the habitat and the creatures that live there, they sometimes cannot figure out what kind of animal this could be. They have brought their recordings of these vocalizations to expert zoologists for analysis. Most of the experts that analyze these recordings will confirm if they are a known species indigenous to the area such as coyote, fox, owl, mountain lion, etc. Some zoologists will analyze something that they have never heard before and cannot come to the conclusion of what species it could possibly be - analysis unknown.

LEGEND MEETS TRUTH

Author and Bigfoot researcher, Ron Morehead

I have never heard the vocalizations of Bigfoot, perhaps I will someday, I can only hope. Ron Morehead has heard the music of Bigfoot and has studied this for many years. This is his story.

The Sierra Sounds Story
By Ron Morehead

Stretching across the Pacific Northwest is the Sierra Nevada mountain range. These mountains support an abundance of wildlife, and also support a mystical creature who continues to stealthily roam that wilderness. He's known as Bigfoot.

A group of six hunters encountered a family of these creatures and captured their vocalizations on cassette recordings. Those recordings are known as the Sierra Sounds. The story is unique, controversial, and mystical in its collectiveness. I was one of those hunters.

Many have gleaned ideas from the Sierra Sounds story; have tried their own ideas in the field, and some have actually experienced these creatures first-hand. But we are still left to wonder - what are they? The Sierra camp chronicle is a time-tested narrative which represents a very big, bipedal, sentient being who interacted with humans. To my knowledge nobody has been around these creatures, tried to trick them more, or understand them better than I have and I still don't know what they are. However, I believe them to be sentient, cognizant thinkers like us. Could that be true? From my experience, it is. But, could there be more? With all our technology and all the folks trying to get a handle on these creatures, how have they remained so elusive for so long?

The Sierra Sounds recordings are unique. They were made

spontaneously and were captured by several of us over a period of several years. They have been studied by the University of Wyoming, professionally analyzed by a retired Naval crypto-linguist, and a complex language has been found in the recordings. Humans are the only ones supposed to actually have language.

In 1971, when the hostile-sounding vocalizations began at our remote hunting camp, we were all a bit edgy, but didn't have to shoot our way out -- although at first that certainly crossed our minds. The aggressiveness of the sounds and the sheer volume coming from these entities was at first very unsettling. At any time we thought they could crash through our make-shift shelter, destroy us with a single blow, and our big guns may not give the desired effect. But we were certainly ready to use those guns. That petrified life-threatening feeling is something I'd never felt before.

After a few more encounters I figured they probably weren't going to harm us – big bark, but no bite. So, I relaxed a little and began to think of their presents as a kindred-type spirit. Perhaps that aggressiveness may not be directed at us. What did they want? Our food? They certainly took what we left out for them but never bothered to take our hanging deer, nor did they bother our stored food that we kept in the ringed barrels that we packed in on mules.

Although they began interacting with us in 1971, they only did it while we were inside the shelter. It wasn't until the late evening of 1974 when Bill McDowell and I actually received an array of interaction while we were outside the shelter. Could this be the night when we'll capture a picture of one? In the past we tried on many occasions to obtain a picture. It soon became apparent that these creatures have the ability to reason and maybe see through our tricks. Although we saw glimpses of these giants, they always remained shy and extremely elusive, only giving us the recordings and their huge casted footprints to go home with.

Never had they been as bold as they were in 1974. Bill and I thought for sure it would only get better from there. But what do they want with us, or from us? They are certainly trying to communicate, but what are they saying? That has been, and still is, my question. The close-in interaction stopped in 1976 when Bill and I were threatened by a bear and had to shoot it. Since then only brief distance chatter, a few sightings, and an occasional tell-tale sign is all we get.

When will we get more answers? Besides the CDs offered on my website **www.bigfootsounds.com**, I've also written the book *Voices in the Wilderness*. My story spans forty years of exploration into the wilds of the Sierra Nevada Mountains of California, attempting to solve the mysteries that surround these giants who have remained extremely enigmatic. I've also travelled extensively, interviewing folks that claim encounters, and have coupled some of the more credible accounts together with my own experiences. Thus, I think I've established a profile which is frank, honest, and hopefully helpful to others. However, it may only be helpful if one has an open mind and is not 'fixated' inside a predetermined paradigm.

Many mysteries about these giants still remain unanswered by classical science. The Sierra camp story still holds several of those unanswered questions. Are they really flesh and blood? They certainly leave big footprints and have a big voice. Is there a paranormal aspect to the enigma? Many believe so. Could quantum physics answer some of these questions and possibly bring all the data together? I think; 'maybe', 'could be', 'perhaps', 'it's conceivable'.

Wood Knocking

The theory is that wood knocking is a form of communicating with either family members or other Bigfoot over long distances. It may be a way for them to locate one another, or perhaps used to warn other Bigfoot in the area that someone is entering into their territory. I have done some wood knocking with good results. Normally I will do wood knocking in three consecutive knocks and then I will wait several moments for a response. You definitely have got to be patient. If you don't get a response right away, it may be because he is checking you out or maybe there are no Bigfoot in the area.

Methods for Searching

Everybody has their own methods of searching for this elusive creature. Some methods I don't agree with, such as taking a large group or a group of loud mouths. I think that the larger the group the less chance you have for finding evidence of Bigfoot and the greater the risk of human contamination. Someone may end up putting their boot print in what could have been a perfect Bigfoot cast. As for the loud mouths, that's all you hear is their loud mouth! When I go out in the field, I want to feel with all my senses. I feel like I am home when I am in the woods and in my element. This creature is curious and will come to you if you just be patient.

Busting your way through his territory will just make him retreat. Going in with fireworks doesn't work either. I have seen that method done before and I just shook my head in disbelief.

Coyotes and Bigfoot

Many researchers have found that Bigfoot and coyotes coincide with each other. They seem to work together with the respect of whom is higher on the food chain. This creature has its own way of doing things in its environment and knows where the game is and will respond to the yips of the coyotes that the game is near. When a coyote gets a fresh kill the pack will yip and howl with excitement. I do not believe that Bigfoot will eat rotting food, and prefers fresh food. They are thought to be omnivorous. Bigfoot has many human aspects and I know that he is very much like us. I believe that coyotes and Bigfoot have a common respect for each other just like humans and man's best (canine) friend.

Gifts from Bigfoot

I have heard many different accounts of Bigfoot leaving a gift for a human. I only received a rock, but it was a nice rock. This testimony that I have heard is surreal. This is a story that a good friend had told me.

This person has a corn field and farm in Ohio. One day he noticed that some of his ears of corn were snapped off. He assumed perhaps some people were coming in and stealing his corn. He wasn't happy about this because this was his livelihood. He went out and saw that there were very big prints - bare footprints. They measured about 18 inches in length and about 9 inches in width. He also noticed a branch with a flower braided and intertwined and just placed where his corn was missing. If it were a Bigfoot leaving behind this gift in return for corn, this just proves that Bigfoot can be a loving and sensitive being.

Trap Cams

Many researchers use trap cameras (also called trail cameras) in the field with the hope that maybe, just maybe, Bigfoot will walk in front of it and it would snap a picture of the unsuspected being. I have worked with trap cams in the past with no results, however it doesn't mean that they don't work. My theory is that Bigfoot can see the Infrared Sensor (IR). The IR flashes a small light and some trap cameras will make a slight clicking sound. This creature lives in the wilderness and if he comes upon something that is not natural or out of the ordinary, it can make him suspicious and wary of getting too close. This is just my own theory and I am sure that this will stir up some controversy with a lot of researchers in the Bigfoot community.

The Cut Through - Power Lines

Also called straightaways, the power lines of North America go through all the states and most of the time are only accessible by foot, horses, or ATV. These are access roads and trails for the workers of the power grid for repairs and or sometimes fire roads. They are also the path of least resistance for wildlife and maybe even Bigfoot. Although some of the cut through does go into the cities and some backyards of the people who live there, for the most part they are untouched. Or are they?

Stereotypical Bigfoot

The stereotype is that Bigfoot is always 8 feet tall and its footprints should always be 17" or more. Are we born 8 feet tall with feet 17 plus in length? I sure hope not! There would be no population of human or Bigfoot. We are born small and when other people say "Well it was a kid in a hoodie", I get a little upset! Why can this not be a juvenile Bigfoot? I have seen smaller footprints that didn't have the same characteristics of a human print. A human foot is more defined in length and width, also with some curves and an arch. Bigfoot has different features in its foot. They are wide and almost square in shape. I am no podiatrist, but I am getting to know and learning the difference between a human print and a Bigfoot print.

This creature also varies in hair color. They are not all dark brown or black. There have been many reports of a white Bigfoot that has been seen here in Rhode Island. The one that I had seen was brown, but just like humans the hair varies in color, so does Bigfoot's. As we get older our hair color changes to grey or white and I believe that the white haired Bigfoot could very well be an older creature.

Shooting B-Roll

During another excursion, Kris and I visited the Tomaquag Indian Memorial Museum in Exeter, Rhode Island on June 29th 2011. We are both of Native American descent and were learning more about the history of the Narragansetts. Also, we had heard that there were some strange things going on in the area. While we traveled down the long dirt road to visit the museum, we had noticed a cemetery that we thought we would like to stop at on the way back. We also thought that it would be a great place to film some of the wooded area, getting b-roll (extra footage) for our documentaries. After we visited the museum, we began to drive back on the dirt road through the heavily-wooded area. It had taken us at least ten minutes to drive down the road to get to the museum, and we expected the same amount of a drive back. Kris was driving very slow so that we could explore the woods as we drove and take in the area. Kris drove just as slow on the way back, stopping after about a minute to grab the camera from the trunk to shoot b-roll footage and also so that we would have it to film a little at the cemetery. I held the camera out the window, film-

Video captures something in the woods.

ing the woods as we slowly drove by. I had only filmed for about a minute when we both realized that we were at the end of the dirt road and almost back onto the main road. Kris and I were perplexed as to how we could have reached the end of the road so quickly, completely missing the cemetery, when it had taken us well over ten minutes to travel the road the first time going about the same speed. The rest of the drive, both Kris and I felt like we were in a fog, not quite right. It almost felt as though we had lost space and time the way we ended up at the end of the road so quickly. I had spent the night at Kris' house that night to go through the video to see if they could use some of the b-roll for our documentaries. What we had found was astonishing! I noticed in the video what appeared to be something walking from behind a tree. Kris and I went over and over the footage and could not debunk it. I had said to Kris, "Oh wow! I think this could be Bigfoot! I can't believe it!" But we could not confirm this on our own, so Kris and I decided to forward the video to a few others that we know and trust in the field to see if they could try to debunk the video. No one had an answer as to what it could be. Some Native American Indians believe that Bigfoot might possess mystical powers or abilities, such as putting humans in a hypnotic trance and thereby remaining invisible. Maybe this is why I didn't see this creature at the time I was filming and Kris and I felt like we were in a fog.

Animal Planet's Finding Bigfoot

After sharing the video clip with one of my team members, to my surprise, he shared this with Animal Planet's TV show Finding Bigfoot. I wasn't very happy about this but what was done was done. The producers had contacted me about doing the show and reluctantly, I agreed to do it. Nothing against the show, I just wanted to keep the video clip to myself for awhile. Bigfoot and my sighting are very personal, and to have what could possibly be a Bigfoot on that video clip was exciting. Working with the filming crew was a nice experience, and they were good to us. I mostly enjoyed going out in the field with Cliff Barackman and Tyler Bounds. Since the taping, we have stayed in contact with Tyler. He has become a good friend of ours and we all get together on occasion.

Are Bigfoot Smarter Than Humans

From what I have observed in my research and talking with other people in the study of Bigfoot, this creature seems to be highly intelligent and has been smart enough to avoid us and the scientific community. Do I think they are more intelligent than humans? In some ways I do. These creatures are elusive and can survive under the most extreme conditions. Most people today are no longer adapted to the natural environment. We are too self-absorbed and surviving out in the elements would kill off most. We as humans can't live without Facebook or an iPhone, never mind electricity and heat.

Smart Enough, At Least, Not To Be Found...
By Carl L. Johnson

Bigfoot, on the whole, doesn't appear to be much of an engineer. Its tool-making abilities probably are equal to that of the great apes. This assessment is based on no researchers claiming to find evidence of Bigfoot having fashioned even rudimentary tools. There are indications that like the great apes, they build temporary nestlings that provide some shelter. They might leave signs for others of their kind, such as broken trees, branches arranged in structures resembling teepees, and rock pilings. Chimpanzees, gorillas, orangutans and baboons will use grass and reeds to pull tasty termites from stumps.

It is quite likely Bigfoot hands possess dexterity superior to the aforementioned apes. Certainly the big, wedge-shaped, bipedal feet revealed by tracks are more human, though seemingly structured for supporting massive weight. If they do use wooden clubs, sticks for stabbing or stones crafted with a cutting/slicing edge, they must be careful to take those implements along with them and not to drop any. (Or, don't we recognize some scattered sticks and chipped stones as Bigfoot tools?) I haven't heard any reports of seeing a Bigfoot in the Americas carrying an object that can be construed as a tool.

I'm not denigrating Sasquatch's relative intelligence. Perhaps their brain power, while rather limited compared to homosapiens, is specialized and chiefly devoted to concealment skills, negotiating their trails through the forests, finding others of its' species, and feeding itself through simpler but effective methods. Harnessing fire – it is surmised this skill was first achieved by our remote antecedents Homo Erectus -- might be beneficial if not essential to Bigfoot, were it not for rendering them far more detectable. I would suspect those creatures have an instinctive dread of fire, seeing it is bright, not of their making and maybe even aware of the danger of forest fire which could drive them into more open territory where they are vulnerable. It could be that Bigfoot knows as much as it can, and as much as it needs to!

Quoting Dina Palazini: *"The smartest creature is the one that remains undiscovered."*

That most, maybe all mammals dream seems fairly obvious. What might Bigfoot dream about; hunting and gathering? Finding a mate? It's family? What of another of its kind with whom it shared a relationship, but who has left or died? If the creature buries its dead, as some Bigfoot researchers contend, it might even regard death with solemnity, seeing the body of one of their own deceased. As with so much about this elusive, almost mythical being, we can only speculate.

Sasquatch!

You might be wondering why I didn't use the term Sasquatch throughout this book? Maybe because some people twist the name Sasquatch around and I don't find the term "squatchy" to be the correct terminology to represent this creature.

Legend Meets Truth

The truth is out there. Through the dedication of all the researchers and their findings the realities behind these legends will begin to surface.

What is essential is establishing effective communication for the exchange of information and sharing experiences.

Let us continue to move forward with our explorations, taking a cooperative approach, our prime directive being discovery.

SOURCES

(1) http://en.wikipedia.org/wiki/Yeti

(2) http://www.dem.ri.gov/programs/bnatres/forest/pdf/riforest.pdf

(3) http://en.wikipedia.org/wiki/Rhode_Island

(4) http://www.visitrhodeisland.com/what-to-do/bird-watching-and-nature-walks/1523/great-swamp-management-area/

(5) http://www.gcbro.com/RIwash0001.html

(6) http://www.visitrhodeisland.com/what-to-do/beaches/491/george-washington-management-area/

(7) http://www.oregonbigfoot.com/report_detail.php?id=00516

(8) http://en.wikipedia.org/wiki/Decomposition

Credits and Special Thanks

A special thank you to:
Thomas Finley "The Cryptid Aritst" for his beautiful book cover and interior artwork.
For more information about Thomas Finley, contact him at capteasycheese@gmail.com or on Facebook at www.facebook.com/thomas.finley.96

A special thank you to:
Kris Stepney for her skills in editing and putting this book together. If it wasn't for her this book would still be just a manuscript.
For graphic design requests contact Kris at KrisStepney1@gmail.com

Thank you to all the eyewitness accounts and testimonies for their contributions to this book:

Greg Best
Aryes Clague
Cody Ray DesBiens
Dylan Fuller
Carl L. Johnson
Ron Moorhead
Kris Stepney

LEGEND MEETS TRUTH

For more information, visit:

www.BigfootSeekers.com
www.BigRhodey.com
www.BeyondTheVeilParanormal.com